Caramel Conscience

Unfeigned Poesey

Deepanjali Sharda

BookLeaf Publishing
India | USA | UK

Made with ❤ on the BookLeaf Publishing Platform

www.bookleafpub.in

www.bookleafpub.com

Dedication

To my parents and grandparents—thank you for passing down wisdom, patience and the genes, literary and otherwise.

To my mother, for always cheering me on, no matter how bizarre the poem.
And to my father, for enduring my literary experiments, offering brutally honest critiques, and managing to smile through my endeavours.

To my brother, husband, and son—thank you for being an endless source of inspiration, eye-rolls, and poetic gold. Whether by accident or design, your antics, conversations, and existence have filled far more pages than you realize.

Preface

Caramel Conscience

Inside my turbulent mind
A voice sticky-sweet and kind,
Whispers in tones of golden gloss—
A soft temptation,
prodding me across.

Telling me that Life is meant to melt,
Not always weighed, not always dealt
With rigid rules or sugar bans—
So, taste the joy, lick the pan

And then it shifts, a gentle nudge,
"Remember balance, don't just indulge.
The sweetest things, though rich and fine,
Can tip the scale if you cross the line."

So here I stand, spoon in mid-air,
With caramel truth and half-aware
That pleasure needs its patient guide—
A conscience dipped, but not denied

Poetry for me has been a way to seize fleeting moments and pen down the thoughts and emotions in colourful tapestry. This poesy is a mosaic of such moments, memories and sentiments united by the restless curiosity that moves us to observe, imagine, and reflect.

The poems here capture the essence of a quiet introspection and ordinary sights seen through a tilted lens. Some are playful, some solemn, and others utterly spontaneous—each born from the impulse to capture something otherwise lost in passing.

There is no roadmap or a promise of order. Just a series of windows inviting you to enjoy a different mood, a new scene or a philosophy. I hope you find something that you can relate to, something that surprises you or even find something you didn't know you were looking for.

Welcome.

Acknowledgements

Acknowledgements

First and foremost, a grand, poetic bow to you—the reader. Whether you're here by fate, accident, or the lure of a pretty cover, thank you for spending your precious time with these verses. If even one line made you smile, sigh, or squint thoughtfully into the distance, then this little book has done its job. Without your curious eyes and open heart, these words would just be thoughts wandering aimlessly.

To my wonderfully patient family, indulgent friends, and learned teachers—thank you for guiding motivating and believing in me. Your support has been my emotional espresso shot, keeping me going when the blank page stared back with too much sass. Your encouragement was the wind beneath my metaphorical wings.

A big cheer and applause to the poets and writers whose work lit the path and reminded me how magical words can be. Even while expressing themselves they allowed my imagination to soar. Your brilliance made me both inspired and mildly envious—and that, dear friends, is the perfect recipe for creation.

And finally, a reluctant thank-you to the quiet moments, awkward silences, 3 a.m. overthinking sessions, and existential spirals that provided endless content. They were unpredictable co-authors, but effective nonetheless.

This book is a patchwork of chaos and calm, scribbled between life's errands and emotional detours. And now, I gift it to you with gratitude, a grin, and maybe a typo or two that slipped past my best intentions.

1. Eternal

Faint hints of scents
A strand of hair every now and then
Making the heart skip a beat
Little acousma reminding of them

Smiles and Laughter
Cuddles and cheers
All that remains is reminiscing and tears

A memory or a dream
Surreal and yet it was
Flesh and bones
With strengths and flaws
Touched and felt
Soft and harsh
Heard and spoke
Saw and loved
Every moment a delight it was
It's a wonder where it disappeared
in all this chaos

What is and still lingers on
Precious words, kind acts of care
A deep fondness that we shared
Little gifts and blessings
Unconditional love, all forgiving
It all once was
Close and right here
Warm and so near
Wishing once again for it to appear

Linking our realities
Are the things that were said
Stories that were shared
Potions that were mixed
Making the circle of life a truth
Sharing the same stories with generation next
Similar tics, leaving us perplexed
Seeing the same spots on the newer member
That were once comforting and tender
It is beautiful how it all still remains
In a new form, in fresh domains

2. Mind Nevermind

Reality is the Truth
and Truth is facts
A belief so common
It's all the magic it lacks
Science logic, maths
proving what is known
looking for the unknown

It's mind boggling, the way mind plays
Surpassing all logic
It's very foundation it sways
It answers the questions
yet questions the answers
proves the reality
yet breaks out doubt like cancers
Here and now is what you see
But what you don't know you will never see
Round and round in circles it takes me
My reality may never be yours
and yours may never be me

A change in perspective changes the scene
a change in tone, shade, fragrance
Maybe all the change it needs
A narration alters the hearing
the mood alters the understanding
so does learning and unlearning
and maybe so goes the saying
CHANGING WITH THE WINDS ALLOWS GROWING
complicated and confusing
mystified, slowly revealing
Is this the story of life
from end to the beginning?
Looking for the truth
but whose?
Just floating with life wherever it goes
or fighting the current and venturing to unknown shores
many lives, many stories, many realities
MIND over body and Soul

3. Devotion

Opening the heart completely
Cherishing each moment fondly
Going beyond logic, believing without a doubt
Unable to answer questions, simply mesmerized is a
Devout

From grandma's tales to the High priest's hymns
From just a look or a presence or a light
The joy and peace take wings
Almighty or a mortal
a task or a puzzle
Something beyond the mind, body and soul
Completely engulfing the human as a whole
Every challenge acceptable, every gesture honoured
even in the darkest hour, hope doesn't grow smaller

The calm in the depths of the Ocean of Devotion
the tranquillity in the madness of obsession

Only the true feel, the ones who comply
Their love is the strength on which they rely
Ever welcoming the celebrations
Embracing all acts of the creation
Accepting as is - the Gospel Truth
Nothing dispelling the faith
Nothing shaking the root
Pure magnetism, such is the lure
Raw passion, of which there is no cure

Calling it an addiction is tainting
So powerful, so pure
It's engulfing, it's a Calling
Emotional, physical, mental
connecting now with eternity
The true essence of spirituality
Coming into yourself, finding yourself
accepting and believing in yourself
Unabashedly surrendering to the power with or without
the drama
Maybe that is heaven, that is Nirvana

Magical is the power of devotion
Be it a mother's love, blind faith, hard work or a lover's
attention

It opens the doors no one envisions
Shrinks the universe, fades all the divisions
Who is the devotee devoted to?
Who is the ardent follower revering?
Is it seeking something external?
It is the happiness and peace inside that's eternal
Many forms, many names, many acts, many meanings present
Devotion is the only way to ascend.

4. New Year

The vibrancies of dusk and dawn
a beautiful tapestry the sky adorns
from grey to blue and orange to gold
it's magical, be the weather hot or cold

The same sun, the same sky and earth
and yet presenting a different time and worth
Break of dawn gets a new hope, new life , a new day
At dusk for many, it's the end of the old way
Not that the night has less to offer
It's a sky full of stars, silver moonlight and a breeze a
little cooler
Yet, after a night full of celebrations and fervour
Everyone cheers and welcomes a new year

It did take the day to follow the dark night
The time that kept ticking, the resilience of light
Proving time and again how fickle is life
The only option is to move on and take it all in a stride

Going from counting the last seconds to waking up to a
fresh sunrise
Harbinger of hopes, change and new beginnings
It's not just the calendar, it's a fresh new innings
Whether or not the reality, the present take a turn
Somehow the heart anticipates, wishes and yearns
for the happiness to flow,
the smiles to grow
the peace to sustain
calm and tranquil to remain
for the eagerness to drive on
the courage to be strong
the belief to be unshaken
uninhibited, opportunities to be taken

It's another winter day in the North
Cold and brutal nip in the air
But don't be fooled, because no matter how it may
appear
It heralds aspirations and cheers

5. Ram Tum Aoge Kya?!

In an era of discoveries
In a decade of growth
Humanity has leapt to love newer luxuries
And humanity has fallen to loathe

Curiosity and looking beyond the seen
From dark ages to fighting for justice
Working on newer avenues we are keen
Yet, here we are
Still intoxicated with war
My God is bigger than yours
My acts in name of religion more mature
And my Divinity?
It's all twisted and obscure

God men and women establishing their brand of law
It's ironic how ignorant ancestors are called barbarians
And the so called ' Scientific Minds'
Don't even see the flaw
Mosque or temple they ask

Insecure?
Power Hungry?
Small Minded?
Why was choosing that difficult a task?
Show of strength? And for what?
God doesn't need a saviour
But religion does

Ayodhya today is a pilgrim hub
The land where Ram came
where Ram remained and still does
The Supreme Being, the ideal human
Dharma personified
brought back from tents to a palace
And we pat our backs
With sin laden hearts, is this enough to cover our tracks?

We rejoice, we establish faith
We bow our heads and pray the evil will fade
Now that Ram's here, righteousness will prevail

No one for a second stopped to think
In a world succumbing to our evils
Does He want to begin a sequel?
Will He again wage a war for Truth?

Offering beautifully ornate palace and throne

Millions chanting His name
With a country filled with hopes
Will it start anew?
Imbibe the Truth, Dharma- the virtue?
Will He really come back in our hearts again?
Ram- Hey Ram Tum aaoge Kya?

6. Infinite Colours

INFINITE COLOURS
A prayer for the higher power
to thank and cherish the senses given
Absolutely a delight to feel the world
It's because of them curiosity exists
and forward we are striven

Oh! how wondrous to be able to
touch and taste
hear, smell and see
Everyone's still enamoured everyone will agree
But what catches the eye
is the magic of colours roll by
It's not all black white or grey
A whole new tapestry is everyday
From dawn to dusk, the world changes
Bright blues to shimmering orange, the sky re arranges

Joyous shades in the spring
Emerald greens during the rains

Earthy hues cheering the autumn
Vivid palettes colouring the summer heat
and cosy greys of winter days
The nature to the eyes is a treat
And what of us?! You and me?
As far as the eyes can see
Scintillating, flamboyant, psychedelic
mute, calm and lively
Mysterious, overwhelming is the world around me

Even the dark brings out shades
A matter of time, adjustments it takes
To appreciate the blacks, the greys
A realm that is real
A realm that is palpable
In our hearts with colours it stays

Through the constant commotion of colours
The hustle-bustle that sometimes is a puzzler
There is a black and white need indeed
to bring us strength and courage
to appreciate the calm, endeavour to be a sage

It's a colourful world
A colourful life
Humbles the human mind
The beauty of the universe

from the beginning to the end of time
Tied up neatly with all the shades
Yet surprising the mind
losing to understand, losing all its crusades.

7. Colour Me

Pick a colour
Tell me what is me?
It's as confusing as it can be
Have you ever chosen,
then re- chosen and again simply changed your mind?
Has it ever been when you just can't decide?
As simple a thing as picking a colour
has almost made me lose my mind

Dreaming of shades and anxiety cutting in like blades
Thinking of White, ethereal and a complete delight
and then Yellow, sunshine, making the world bright
Orange, Peach or Pink
Which one's my favourite I just can't think
Red is love, red is passion
colour of hearts, never out of fashion
Colours for a princess for a queen
the royal Purple, the earthy green
and what about the limitless Blue
Which one's me, I have no clue

Maybe Grey or bold Black
Deciding on one is what I lack
Please cut me some slack
and let me hang on to my Rainbow
Drown in my colours
as per my moods and as my whims go

8. Wisdom

Looking at the world outside
Distracting from the mundane life
A sight caught my eye
Surprised pleasantly
and still feeling a pang of jealousy
Caught off guard snapped out of my confusions
There it was, a little smile full of joy
A calm appearance
Proof of a content mind
Amidst the real chaos
finding a space and time
Grateful for the moment
for the breaths and the nourishment
Not in an ambiance or a service that is starred
Right there on the roadside
giving dust, traffic, noise a complete disregard
Taking precious moments from a tight schedule
This person seemed to be running on a different fuel
A thought hit me so hard
cutting through the webs of mind like a shard

Nothing and no one can get the peace I seek
Luxuries and temptations had made me weak
The greed in me wasn't letting me grow
Entangled in my own misconceptions,
into the river, diamonds I throw
What has he to gloat
no materialistic things, no power to boast
And yet, it's me wreathing with pain
while he is happy and sane
Like a wakeup call was this momentary sight
How I had robbed me of the light and delight
Nowhere is the race taking anyone
There is no place else to be
Have no regrets and find inner peace
All wise men have conceded
Nothing else in the end is needed

9. Hurtful Love

It is strange
Wonder why I stopped talking to you
Should I be guilty?
For reaching out to you
With my problems, my issues
my insecurities
My dilemmas, struggles
responsibilities
Once was enough to seek help
and be dissociated
Don't know why i keep hoping still
Knowing you won't help

It's on me i guess
To love till I am broken
To love till I am loveless
It's a fear I still have
To be cold and alone
When there is so much to give
Yet anger eats me to the bone

Angry at myself
To seek you in happiness and despair
In highs and lows
In fights and in peace
It's you I seek

It's too much to ask for you to change
Is it too much to ask for a hug?
a smile?
Letting me know you are by my side?
It's strange
How paths change
Walking side by side and pushing each other away
With such a mess in my heart and brain
It is strange
How I am still fighting for us
Coz the heart refuses to let go
Battered it's still beating your name
And like an incorrigible moron
I keep choosing you again and again

10. Strength in YOU

It's times when everything is dark
Possibilities and opportunities at best seem stark
The dues are much higher
The credits get bleaker
The days are long and nights full of fear
That's when you need you the most
Believing in yourself will make you stay afloat
Take a pause, breathe in deep
It's alright to break down, allow yourself to weep
But don't let yourself give up
Don't you quit
It is life, it will get overwhelming
Each breath, each moment may seem draining
Remember ' This too shall pass'
It always will be, it always was
Nothing is permanent, be grateful for that
For you were happy earlier, don't forget that
Time will move on bringing in the change
It hurts and it heals, it sure is strange

So when wounded, know the remedy is near
Just love yourself, wait for things to clear
Ask, if it all ends here, will you have peace and no
regret?
Ask, if you did give it your all, gave it your best?
It's after the darkest minute the dawn breaks out
In complete chaos, clarity comes about
Allow yourself to float awhile
Let the shores pass you by
It's not the end, life is seeking
It's a journey, through twists and turns it's raking
The troubles, the struggles, the demons everyone has to
face
Don't make it a competition or a race
Be thankful, and enjoy it at your own pace
So when you are lonely, fearsome and weak
Know that it's time for you to just be
Love is the cure, allow it to engulf you
Be kind to yourself, for this life is All About You!!

11. Nomad's Life

What will happen after death?
A mystery that shrouds all our minds
For no one knows what is beyond
Yet, for an afterlife we go through daily grinds
Civilizations have gone by
Historians have given different reviews
Archaeologists are still perplexed
But paradise is everyone's favourite muse

So here's a little story
that matches my theory
About someone who lived, loved life king size
Wanderer, sharp, creative, adept and wise
Someone rare to find
A beautiful soul and mind
For even after bidding adieu
Had a request for the closest few
To take around the ashes
Allow one last journey
Even though idea got some lashes

The remains were evenly packed and scattered
In the places that mattered

One part however had an adventure of its own
From being lost in a car, to being stolen
finally landed at the right spot
that an entire establishment looked for and sought
The soul wanderlust and scrappy
Hopefully is now at peace and happy
Inspiring me even more
To write down so no one can ignore
For me in the beyond I see
is the traveller I longed to be
With all the lemons that life gave
This nomad I have somehow saved
Tomorrow or maybe someday
I'll get to see it all my way

And just in case I don't
This back up plan of mine should work
If not in flesh blood and bones
then why not in an urn?
Or scattered away in the wind?
Free like a bird, un-coffined
It is funny and sad
How I am betting on the unknown
Instead of making a change that is rad

I am simply unwilling to own
Priority needs a shake
Choices and plans need a remake
This is the life, now and here
It's either this moment or no where.

12. Self Love

Every second every moment struggling to even fight
Fixed and helpless, speechless with fright
No light to see at the end of the tunnel
Digging, breaking rocks, but it's useless to pummel
The thoughts come and stay
All about being alone and betray
No beautiful sight or sound lets them sway
Here's a mind that has gone astray
Forgetting the times when there were smiles
No matter how hard, never counting the miles
The times when all was well
Protected with an invisible shell
Nothing could dampen the mood
Small setbacks the heart would soothe
Now, it doesn't really matter
The mind is broken, it's in tatters
The heart weeps, it beats even faster
The world, the life, it's a disaster
Don't worry, this is not the end
There is only one cure, to mend

Let it all go for a while
Breathe,
don't stop these thoughts that are vile
Instead let them fly by
Don't latch on let them flow out, cry
They are a storm
They will cause havoc
They are quick sand
You forever will be stuck
Wait a while, things will change
for they always do
Brace for the worst, hope for the best
Love yourself, just be there for you.

13. Woman

Here's a story
of Pride and Glory
Standing against all odds
Defying the holy and the Gods
Story of a life
Supressed, barely allowed to survive
Used and manipulated in ways
Bearing burdens till this day
Love, care and nurture filled
Supporting empires to build
Made to feel small and weak
Taught to hide, be meek
Called a fool, learning taken away
Easiest target, easy prey
Slaving and accepting a fate
Killing hopes of a better day
Last breaths were difficult to take
She then looked around
Seeing many like her shook her ground
Realizing she was a life

For her daughters and others, she took a strive
All the shackles and chains came undone
Once she stood for all and one
Struggled, fought, made her space
From taking baby steps to running full pace
Sometimes with love
Sometimes with war
She kept rising and raising the bar
It's been a journey, with many scared even now to
embark on
But the freedom it brings is getting impressed upon
Still many hope and wish they were him
One day completely squashed will be this whim
Proud to be the spirit, the soul of the world
She brings magic, the life to this world.

14. Smile

An upward curve from ear to ear
or just a crecent on the face
A smile can say it all or everything it can stow away
A delight, happiness and cheer
Grinning and laughing coz the high spirit can't be
contained
Infectious the giggles are, bringing out emotions
unchained
The all-knowing, patiently observing
Adorn themselves with a smirk
Some can't decipher, while others feel the irk
Pretending to be there, while the mind wanders
Keeping a slight beam
Intrested they seem
Pleased with themselves, enjoying the moment
Simpering, hiding from the appreciation
Shying away from the attention
With pride and joy, beaming
Is a smile with happy tears streaming
Making the dreams a reality

Watching the prayers, the hard work, the perseverance
come to life
And then there is the blatant lie
Concealing the hurt, stifling the cry
Posing to be brave while their world falls apart
Blocking the ignominy, protecting the battered heart
A smile is an expression
An everlasting impression
From bringing people closer
To being a conniving poser
It's the best thing to give to your lips
It can always lift up the spirits.

15. Mystery Files

Who doesn't enjoy a murder mystery
Digging into characters and their diverse history
A regular mundane day
that went seriously astray
Someone missing,someone dead
some with an alibi, an entagled web
For alot many it's the thrill of how
After hearing about it, can't be a bystander now
Secretly wishing to solve it in real life
What an adventure?! to find tit-bits, a perfume or a knife
Then for some it's a puzzle
Can't snap off and sleep in a befuddle
For even in dreams the events will transpire
Like a new story altogether the mind will inspire
May change tracks
Add people around
feature what it lacks
&by us the case cracks
It's a wonderful thing to dream
One often is the hero, the cherry on the cream

But what about the case at hand
Someone else's imagination
deserves an ending grand
The nitty grittys , the sharp eyes like Holmes
catching hints, twitches, fabric shreds or loam
Interesting it gets
when there is no respite for the suspects
Keeping the audience guessing
to and fro their minds racing
about what they missed while the case was unfolding
Elementary or not, it's thrilling
Nancy or Hardys or the famous five
deeper into the secret they dive
Byomkesh to Poirot to Patrick Jane
unraveling the truth is never in vain
for the evil is prosecuted
and justice survives
endings are enjoyable maybe not so in the real lives
Whodunit? detective sagas , crime fiction
they are truly an addiction

16. A Doctor

A DOCTOR

No one knows better
the plight of a doctor
But the healers themselves
Literally they are the magical elves
Studying all day, working all night
Trying to bring in health, a ray of light
For those who were unfortunate
and also for those who were 'asking for it'
As if that is what studying medicine is about
Self-sacrifice, self-pity and self-doubt
From the book with endless pages
written in a language from the dark ages
To the never-ending queues of patients
An important virtue it imparts- Patience
The seniors scolding and bullying
explained as the only way of practical learning
And along come the googling relatives
changing patients' histories and narratives
so from google, the diagnosis they can match

leaving the doctor second guessing and starting from
scratch
It's a miracle how so many remain sane
In a society confused whether medicine is a boon or a
bane
Magical hocus-pocus, home remedy and tantra -yantra
Everything is acceptable, even chanting Mantra
And when life is finally hanging by a thread
They seek doctors when it's the worst they dread
Expecting cures that are supernatural
And if the healers manage well, it's to God they are
grateful
Don't get me wrong, it's not God we are trying to be
But just have a heart
Trust us and stay healthy
All the blood sweat and tears that we pour in
Let us be proud of it
It's our biggest Win.

17. Tea and Me

The light of joy it brings
and it does literally give you wings
The answer to all fatigue
is a drink full of intrigue
Cold or hot
brewed or not
a few sips, gulps or a lot
all sadness it can blot
Black or green
flowery or lemony
sugared, sugar-free or dipped with honey
with milk and or with all the spices
a drink that can be twisted as per vices
For those who love it
are truly addicted
With or without excuse
always looking to brew
The aroma, the taste, the flavour
an infusion that entices with every layer
For waking up, for pains, for sleeping

It's even for when you are alone or socializing
Someone really had the right notion
Spreading it beyond the ocean
Getting the world together
To a routine adding a little merriment and fervor
Really thank God for tea
How dull without it would life be?!
It hits the sweet spot between spirits and coffee
Moreish yet bringing tranquillity
A teapot full of tea
It works like therapy
Nothing works better for me
than me and my tea

18. The Truth They Should Know

They think they are intelligent
but never understand what a girl meant

They simply call the girls "Complex creatures"
but hoot and whistle when they see shapely figures

Cribbing all day that, "Women cramp our style!"
In the end it's them from whom they want a look, a smile
They act all Oh! all Macho and male
But at the slightest of pain they grow all pale

Wonder why they think, they are God's masterpiece?
Don't they see that after making them God was ill at ease
All uncomfortable because of these hooligans
Who wear dirty socks
Have messy rooms
enjoy cussing rough housing and guns

They can never give or take directions

And everything important they forget to mention
Romancing is beer and take out
or have a candle light dinner when the power is out
They keep bullying the girls
and keep wondering ,"Why do things go wrong with
me?"
It's high time they realized that after all God is a She!

19. Weathered and Fearless

Is it alright to love and loose and fall in love again?
Risk everything, put your heart on the line
even when you know future might be the same?
The same old story
rosy in the beginning and heart wrenching in the end?
Is it alright to gamble in this game of love
when you know there may be nothing to gain?
Loose, yes you may and fall harder than you did before
And maybe this time the sorrow sucks you deeper and
beyond any cure
Is it alright to get pulled in it?
and feel what you are scared of feeling?
Let the colours come back and brighter,
And walk with a hop and step with a zing?
Let go of whatever happened in the past, start fresh?
Let this new love knock on the door and create a new
niche?
To wonder if you are being thought of?
To want to climb the summit, right to the top?
To laugh without a reason, to get excited on small

things?
To want to fly without wings?
Is it actually possible to let your heart feel?
To be confident enough to be able to see it for real
Not be scared of all follies in you and the cost you might
have to pay
Embrace with a beautiful smile, wake up to a new world
and enjoy everyday
Let the moonshine, sunshine and the rainbows fill you
Let the emotions take over and senses heighten, feel like
a rose kissed with dew?
Is it all alright to move on and drown in these waters?
To let it engulf you till nothing else matters?
Love comes in special ways, just give it time
and it grows and matures like a fine wine
Love, that's what we all live for and want
Just like heaven, it's right there
It's a wish, a regard ,a blessing, a prayer.

20. Triumphant Existence

We are born with a purpose unknown
We walk through the dark woods following rays of hope
We succumb to difficulties and still fight till the end all
alone
We grow wiser, grow stronger, overcoming our fears
hanging onto hope
The strands seem weaker and yet we hang on
With every bend and every curve
Often we forget our search
So tied up are we, that from our path we swerve
We want to lead
For others to follow and hold on
Whether we are ourselves adrift
Or in our own battles torn
What is to be looked for?
Is it fame or internal peace?
To remember ourselves or be remembered across seven
seas?
We all are caught in our own webs
Again and again pulled down with the social debts

Saints or humans?
Are we going to be angels or demons?
Scared of evil taking us over
And too selfish to follow the sermons
Here we are living a confused lost life
On hopes, dreams and in search of Truth we thrive
With no clue to where the road leads
trudge through the laid paths and fulfilling our needs
Like a herd of sheep
doltish and ignorant, we let the darkness creep
If it all gets over and we get a chance to see
About one thing everyone will agree
Nothing else but a golden heart matters
faith, love, peace it splatters
Heroes we all are
All equals, all at par
In our own lives we are the lead
May not have odes written in our glory
But that is what we don't even need
Just a loving hand holding ours in the end
Marking our victory!

21. To My Valentine

Cupid took a shot at me a few years ago
Had your name written on the arrow
Took a lot of time to understand and accept
That off my feet indeed I had been swept
Silly me, didn't realize
Like the comfort food, cola and fries
Those chuckle-worthy, dreamy mails you sent
Would have serious side effects
And I would be blinded to all the defects

Not that you are bad at all
I would any day for you take the fall
It's the fact that you are still a mystery
That adds to my misery

I haven't been able to make up my mind
Why is it that I am still so blind?
Marriage is an eye opener, it's true
Yet I still always want to be with you
I wonder if it is right or wrong

A heart that's still singing your song

I just want you to be happy and smiling
Always know that I am right here, Waiting
No matter how far I get
Loving you is something I'll never regret

It's the most precious thing I own
The most perfect, most beautiful element I have known
From loving you to being puzzled
I think I almost doubled everything I had gambled
Honey, you sustain and curb my entropy
It is such an irony
And this does sound clichéd and cheesy
But you are the one who completes me...